Slash
And
Thrust

by John Sanchez

Published by Paladin Press
Boulder, Colorado

Slash and Thrust
by John Sanchez
Copyright © 1980 by John Sanchez

ISBN 0-87364-188-4
Printed in the United States of America

Published by Paladin Press, a division of
Paladin Enterprises, Inc., P.O. Box 1307,
Boulder, Colorado 80306, USA.
(303) 443-7250

Direct inquiries and/or orders to the above address.

Table of Contents

Introduction

There are many who like to indulge in "Knife Trivia". This book was not written for them. It is for the serious student interested in refining his skills. In these pages I do not discuss whether or not the Bowie knife was developed from the Spanish navaja. Nor will you read much here of the historical roots of modern knife fighting. Books, excellent books, have already been published which go into these matters in great detail.

What then is my purpose in writing *Slash And Thrust*?

I feel I have much to say about this martial art that, to my knowledge, has never been said before.

This book is a training aid, no more, or less. Read it, and then assimilate through practice the principles set forth herein.

I. The Martial Knife

In choosing a knife for fighting, the design of the blade demands first consideration. Handle, finger-guard, and artistic merit are of secondary importance when compared to the sharp, durable edge, and the penetrating point of a well-crafted knife.

Blade styles range from that of a Renaissance Stiletto, to that of the Ghurka Kukri. The latter is awkward at best when used for a thrust. The Stiletto is traditionally edgeless. The Kukri and the Stiletto represent the extremes of knife design, and the types that lie between these two number in the thousands. If that class of edged weapons that are used for throwing are taken into account, the varieties of blade shape are just about countless.

Despite this, the martial knife falls into one of three basic categories. It can be made for cutting, thrusting, or both.

At this point we will do well to remember the words of a 16th century swordsman/writer named George Silver: "A perfect fight stands upon both cut and thrust." Although written in reference to the sixteenth century sword duel, this is also true of the modern knife fight.

Neither the knife that sacrifices its edge in order to be the perfect thrusting weapon, nor the dull-pointed knife that is only a fine slasher, are ever chosen by the adept knife fighter.

Again, the common sense of George Silver: "Sometimes (the weapon-hand will) be in a place where you may strike, and cannot thrust without loss of time, and sometimes in a place where you may thrust, and cannot strike without loss of time." There is no reason to limit yourself to a single blade tactic anymore today than during Silver's time.

A good fighting knife, then, will be designed for both cutting and thrusting. This class of knives splits neatly into two basic styles.

Some call the first category the "Bowie Style". But if one gives it this name, what about the knives that belong in this group yet were designed many centuries before the Bowie? A more fitting name for this category is the "Butcher Style."

These knives have broad, sturdy blades, often with a single edge, but always with a serviceable point as well. Examples of this style are the Bowie, Scramasax, Japanese Tanto, Cinqueda, and the Butcher Knife proper.

The second category I call the "Dagger Style". Fighting daggers have rather narrow blades, which are generally double edged. Though of point-oriented shape, the well-made fighting dagger will have at least one sharp edge. The Fairbairn-Sykes is a good representative of this type. A typical variant is the modern Italian Stiletto.

Butcher and dagger are both good styles. Personal preference is the only way to choose between them.

When looking over a prospective fighting knife, take your time. First, examine the blade. Hold it directly under a light, edge upwards. Does the edge catch the light, and reflect as a thin white line over its

4

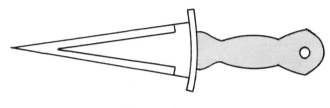

Cinqueda

Stiletto

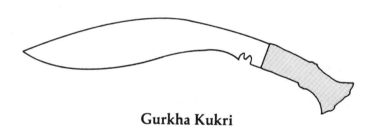

Gurkha Kukri

Fairbairn-Sykes

5

entire length? If so, it was poorly sharpened. Hold it in the same position. Is the edge as sharp toward the point as it is at the middle and rear of the blade? It should be.

Pay close attention to the hand-guard. Its purpose is twofold; to keep your hand from slipping onto the edge when a thrust is executed, and to keep a hostile blade from sliding up and cutting your fingers. Either of these mishaps may mean the end of the fight for you. Avoid pretty, artistic metal work that does not do its job. Determine if the guard is functional.

Consider the handle. It is a bad idea to select a knife with deep finger-grooves, for they will limit you to a single grip. If a situation demands that a different grip be used, a deeply grooved handle can compromise your alternatives.

There are several ways to affix the handle to the tang of the blade. The "full tang" method is the strongest and most durable. Here, two slabs of wood are riveted to a tang that is the same height that the finished handle will be. This is the strongest method of construction. It gives support to the junction of blade and guard, a place where weak knives are prone to bend and break.

There are many variations of handle style, but the Japanese and Saber types are most preferable. When gripped, these handles naturally orient the edge and point in relation to the hand. Make sure that the hilt is long enough. Five inches is about right for the average size hand.

If a Butcher-Style blade is your choice, be sure that the point is capable of easy penetration. If it is not, this fault can often be corrected by grinding an unsharpened false edge on the back of the Butcher blade.

Should you favor the Dagger Style, get a knife with a broad blade. Daggers frequently lack overall strength.

Scramasax

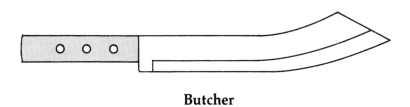

Butcher

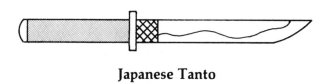

Japanese Tanto

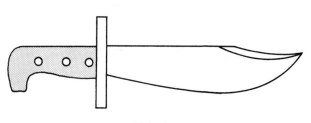

Bowie

HANDLE STYLES

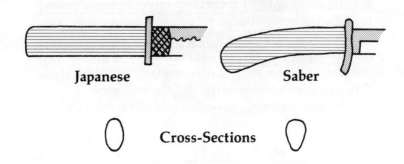

Japanese   Saber

Cross-Sections

TEST CUTTING

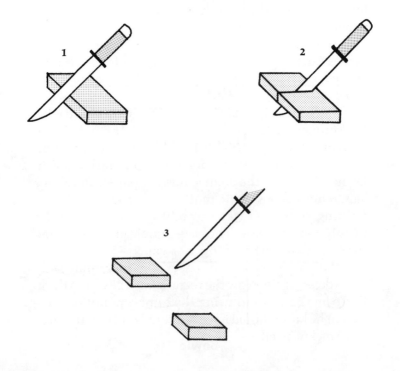

Japanese Blade Test

In feudal Japan, the sword-edge was tested for cutting power. The prospective buyer would demand to know the results before he would purchase the blade. Test-cutting was often done by skilled professionals, called *tameshigiri men*. Cadavers were used in this process, and tales are told of legendary swords that cut through seven bodies with one smooth blow.

Social conditions have changed, yet steel is still the same. How can it be known if an edge is sharp, unless it is subjected to some form of *tameshigiri*? Old methods are impractical, but the following is a trustworthy way. It can be repeated time after time in exactly the same way, which allows one to set up an unchanging standard of sharpness.

Take a sheet of newspaper, roughly 21 inches by 15 inches in size. Fold it 6 times, producing a small rectangle 64 layers thick. With a small C-clamp, fasten the paper to a solid table so that it protrudes two inches over the edge. Take the knife to be tested and mark it 4 inches back from the point. If the blade is strongly curved, measure it on the curve. Touch its edge to the paper at a 45° angle, starting from where the blade edge was marked. Grip the loose end of the paper hard with the thumb and index finger of your left hand. Then, with only medium pressure, stroke the knife through the paper. Apply the same pressure from start to finish. Do not stop until the point leaves the paper, and above all, do not use a sawing motion. If the knife is fit for fighting, it will cut completely through the paper cleanly and with ease. The blade should give the feeling that it is doing the cutting, not you.

Put the two pieces of paper together, and clamp them down again. Now the rectangle is 128 layers thick. Perform the test-cut using the same amount of pressure. The knife should have no trouble cutting through this thickness either.

Blade Length

Seven and one-half inches is a good length for the blade of a martial knife. A few inches less and it will be too short. Those over this recommended size are hard to carry, particularly if they are to be concealed. Which leads to the next subject.

The Carry

There are four ways of carrying a knife in a belt sheath, which is the most common type of knife sheath. All are "open" methods; that is, the knife cannot be concealed.

The knife can be worn on the right hip so that it hangs low on the right thigh, the same way that movie cowboys wear guns. This carry gives a fast draw, but is very noticeable. Furthermore, it smacks of the melodramatic.

You can wear the knife high on the right hip, but this makes for a slow, clumsy draw. The hand tends to grab the knife in an ice-pick grip, with the blade pointing downward from the little-finger side of the fist. If worn high on the left hip, the position of the sheath again provides only an awkward draw.

Of this sort, the best is the inclined belt carry. Here, the sheath is worn on the left side slightly toward the front, with the handle inclined forward. With practice, this position gives the fastest belt draw.

It is customary in the western world to carry the knife with its edge down. The Japanese prefer to wear all bladed weapons edge up. Try both ways with the inclined belt carry, taking notice of the position of your forearm when drawing. Given a right-handed opponent, an edge-down draw exposes the hand and forearm to a disabling tendon cut. The edge-up carry makes its user reach for the knife from the inside. When drawing the knife here, the natural tortion of the body puts the hand and forearm in a hard-to-cut position. Further-

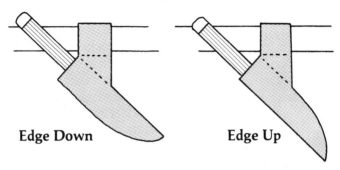

Edge Down   Edge Up

INCLINED BELT CARRY

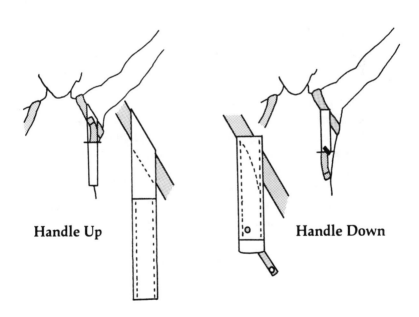

Handle Up   Handle Down

SHOULDER RIGS

more, it is easy to time a cut directly from an edge-up draw. As soon as it clears the sheath, the knife is in a good position to slash out.

Short knives may be carried in a boot, or on the left forearm in a sheath attached to a wrist band. In the forearm carry the sheath must have a restraining strap with a heavy duty snapper. Never use a sheath designed so that the snapper is opened by the index-finger. The snap should be flicked open by the thumb, and the knife drawn in a single motion.

A shoulder holster offers a quick draw and comfortable concealment. I suggest that you don't buy one ready-made; most holsters on the market are made for pistols anyway. Make it yourself and you can be sure of a good fit. This should not take more than fifteen minutes, and can save you upwards of $20.

First check the accompanying diagrams. Use inch wide elastic to form the figure eight; sew the strap where it crosses itself at the back, and where the ends meet. Make it a snug fit. The sheath can be sewn on, or attached by velcro strips if used with a light knife.

The sheath can be pointing either up or down. If the handle-down shoulder carry is desired, the sheath will need a restraining strap. As with the forearm sheath, it should be the type that opens with the thumb.

This carry is perfect when worn under an open jacket. To draw, reach under the jacket, and as your fingers close on the knife hilt, flick the snapper free with your thumb. Now without pausing, pull the knife out, and execute an aggressive attack or defensive maneuver.

The handle-up shoulder carry is best used when a buttoned coat is worn over it. Leave the coat's top two buttons open.

A blade can be concealed in the front right pants pocket. Cut a slit in the pocket's bottom, and push the sheathed knife through until the butt is a half-inch below the pocket's top. Then sew velcro on the back of the sheath and the inside of the pocket to hold the rig in place. Decent sized pockets and full-cut pants legs are necessary here.

It can readily be seen that there is no perfect way to carry a knife. Desirability of concealment, and varieties of clothing determine the sheath system to be used. A good idea is to become familiar with three methods of carrying your knife; one open and two concealed. An excellent selection would be the following: the inclined belt carry, a handle-down shoulder holster, and the pocket carry.

No matter what carry system you choose, work at being comfortable and proficient with it. A little practice goes a long way.

II. Training

For some unclear reason, the subject of knife practice is often slighted, even in those books that claim to give deep attention to it. In this chapter, I present the precepts of the training method that I use. Other systems exist, but the one outlined here is oriented toward both combat reality and personal development. In my opinion, it stands far above the rest in terms of pure usefulness.

It would be foolish to go onto a fencing strip with no experience and hope to defeat a master fencer. No one target shoots without having previously touched a rifle, or pistol, and expects to match the score of a marksman. Yet there are many people who do not realize that training is necessary to be good with a knife.

Perhaps this is due to the fact that the most popular form of edged weapons practice is fencing, a formalized sport. But pure fencing has traded its combat value for civility and etiquette. With such a background it can be hard for modern man to see the part played by aggressive skill and intelligence in a fight with knives, which even when performed with mock weapons is intrinsically savage.

The only way to perceive that knife combat is truly an art, and not mere styleless aggression, is to gain a first-hand acquaintance with your blade, and the type of fighting techniques best suited to its design.

Notice the physical characteristics of your training ground, for they will affect the value of the training performed there.

No one can foretell where they will be called upon to use their knife fighting skills. It could be in an open field, or a narrow corridor. The terrain may be smooth and flat, as in a parking lot, or it may vary from foot to foot as a staircase does. The answer to this is that you must anticipate all situations when practicing. Therefore, if the training grounds are in a natural setting, use small trails to simulate sidewalks. Densely wooded areas, when little underbrush is present, give the feel of rooms with furniture. If you can be aware of a tree three feet behind you without looking, and then react by changing tactics to suit its presence without thinking, you can do the same with a table or chair. Use small elevations to represent the short group of stairs found in front of many buildings; higher ones as full stairways.

If an urban practice area is to be used, do the opposite. Look for terrain features that can strategically represent various kinds of natural features.

As a general rule, do not practice in gymnasiums. Such conditions represent none that you are likely to fight under, whether in the city or country.

A good size for the training ground is three paces wide by ten paces long. This is a multi-purpose size, for it can be adapted to simulate many different kinds of physical situations. There should be obstructions to footwork on both of the long sides, such as sudden rises or drops in elevation, walls, or underbrush.

Prior to starting a practice round, note the distance separating you and your partner. To train in a realistic manner, get used to "squaring off" at both long (12 feet) and short (3 feet) ranges.

The Mock Knife

The mock knife is made of three-eighths inch pine or oak, with a dull point and rounded edges. Its length must be the same as that of your real weapon. The blade style of the martial knife that you carry should be reproduced exactly in your training knife, save that the point must be rounded.

Mock knives made of rubber are available, but these have too much whip in the blade to give realistic contact when used in sparring. The psychological effects of training with rubber weapons can be undesireable also. One can be hit many times with a rubber knife without feeling pain; this can give the student a false sense of invulnerability, and worse yet, a careless attitude.

A wooden knife gives extremely realistic contact. Use of a wooden blade ends all dissent among trainees as to whether or not a "hit" was scored, for a wooden knife lets one know very clearly when contact is made. In addition, it lets trainees know the strength of their cuts and thrusts. This is of critical importance, as the following example will prove.

A light cut on the right triceps will not slow down a determined opponent. At best, blood will be drawn, which he might not notice until the fight is over.

A cut delivered to the triceps with moderate strength may sever the brachial artery, resulting in a true bleeder wound. But this cut would take time to effect the opponent. I know of no one who is good enough to dodge an enemy's slashes for five minutes or so, while waiting for him to weaken from loss of blood.

Now we come to the cut delivered with power and a good follow-through. This cut, on the right triceps,

17

will not only sever the brachial artery, but renders useless the triceps itself. Also, part of the biceps would probably be slashed through. That arm is now out of the fight. It is needless to speak of the severe shock that is attendant upon such gross tissue damage and heavy bleeding.

Do not be satisfied with light, polite contact in training. Be aware of the power of every attack that you make, and always strive to make your moves stronger.

Safety Measures

When sparring in this fashion, small injuries are inevitable. However, their number may be cut down by the minimal use of protective clothing. Heavy gloves and a long sleeved shirt will guard arms and hands from abrasions and bruises. The knees will take many sharp blows, so long pants are a good idea. A scarf or bandana can be worn about the neck, preventing the friction burns that come from high-speed slashes.

In training, do not thrust to the throat, or cut or thrust at the head with contact. These strikes can be fatal, even when delivered with a wooden knife. It could be argued that a mask such as fencers wear would give protection against these blows, thereby allowing their use in sparring. This is true, but the effect of practicing with a fencing mask on is to make you feel uneasy and slightly disoriented when you have to fight without it.

Excluding the three mentioned above, there are no illegal blows in knife practice.

Not counting the few pieces of protective gear, everyday clothing must be worn when sparring. Do not wear sneakers and a sweat-shirt unless you always do so. Leather soled dress shoes do not give good traction, but if they are worn everyday, they must be worn when practicing as well.

If one trains in clothing designed expressly for that

purpose, it is easy to unconsciously associate the action of fighting with the act of wearing this particular style of clothing. This is a bad thing to let happen, for if you have to use your skill, the odds are that you will be wearing street clothing at the time. The effect of this psychological conditioning may cause a momentary hesitation at the very time that you should seize the initiative and attack the enemy. Again, it is highly undesirable to ingrain such tendencies. Every training step that diverges from the reality makes that training more dangerous to the student.

Score Sheets

It is useful to keep a score sheet. On it record the number of bouts in the sparring session, the hits scored in each bout, and the name of the "survivor" of each bout. In the illustration, "Typical Well-Kept Score Sheet," the notes under a trainee's name are the hits that were scored on him by his opponent.

Only those hits that would have effect in real combat are counted. Thus a light cut on a large muscle group would not be recorded. An exception would be if a sensitive target was hit by three or four light slashes in nearly the same spot. In a case like this the cluster of cuts is marked down as one, for they would have the same efffect as a single hard cut.

If a thrust is executed, the same rule applies. Weak, and ill-placed thrusts are not to be counted. As an example, a medium strength direct thrust to the breast bone might gouge the skin in a real fight, but it would be unlikely to achieve penetration to the heart. The value of this particular thrust is nonexistent, even though it would cause some bleeding, and perhaps chip the bone. This blow, if recorded as "heart thrust," would distort the true nature of the fight. Therefore it should not be counted.

The value of the score sheet lies in its use as a

19

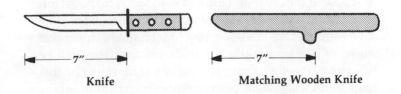

Knife   Matching Wooden Knife

SMITH VS. CONRAD

	Conrad –	Conrad o	Smith –	Smith o	Survivor	Decisive?
1			3 ARMS, LEG		CONRAD	✓
2			2 HANDS		CONRAD	✓
3	1 ARM	1 CHEST	1 LEG	1 ARM	SMITH	INDECISIVE
4			1 ARM	1 KIDNEY	CONRAD	✓
5		1 STOMACH	1 LEG		SMITH	INDECISIVE
6			3 HANDS, LEG		CONRAD	✓
7			1 THROAT		CONRAD	✓
8			3 LEGS, ARM		CONRAD	✓
9			2 ARMS		CONRAD	✓
10		1 STOMACH			SMITH	✓
11			3 HANDS, LEG		CONRAD	✓
12			2 ARMS, LEG		CONRAD	✓
13			2 ARMS		CONRAD	✓
14	2 ARMS				SMITH	✓
15			3 HANDS, ARM		CONRAD	✓

"–" = Cut
"o" = Thrust

WELL-KEPT SCORE SHEET

20

diagnostic tool. Do not look at it to see who is better than whom, but regard it rather as a record of strengths and weaknesses. It is worthwhile to study it, taking notice of both general tendencies and specifics, such as which tactics work for you. Examine it to find personal shortcomings as well. Your opponent can never hit you through his skill. He can only hit you through your own weaknesses. Once these weak points have been recognized, isolate them in your training, and eliminate them by concentrated practice.

When you win a bout, find out why by scrutinizing your own aggression. Then refine your tactics further in the next session.

Give much thought to your individual style between practices, for this is the road to mastery.

III. Knife Fighting

There seems to be a sharp contrast between the previous chapter and this one. Practice versus reality. Yet this contrast, when examined, proves superficial. Training actions takes their form from real combat with steel weapons, and so the two are intertwined. Common sense is all that is needed to make training movements simulate true fighting conditions.

Guard Positions

Knife fighting is a many faceted art. Guard positions will be discussed first. On this subject there are two opposite schools of thought, the old and the modern.

The old concept of the guard was common to medieval Europe and feudal Japan. Here the word "guard" is deceptive, for many of the old fighting positions did not actually protect any part of the body. The guard was defined as "legs, body, hands, and weapon, in readiness to commence action." There were many guard positions, suitable to a wide array of different situations. Most of them were oriented to offense. Guard was changed to conform with the terrain, and the enemy's spirit.

The modern guard concept is well known, for it has been popularized by sport fencing. This states that the guard position should lend itself to parrying, as well as leaving the fencer open to as few attacks as possible. The development of this concept stems from the gradual formalization of European duelling and practice. It is important to realize that in the formal duel, a fencer with a small-sword did not have to use it against a cutlass-fighter, saberman, staff-wielder, or two opponents at once. Likewise, in modern fencing (foil, epee, and saber) the lengths and weights of weapons, size of the fencing strip, and targets areas are limited by complex and restrictive rules. Under such conditions a specialized and defensive concept of the guard has value.

For the knife, however, there are no targets that are off limit, the terrain could be anything imaginable, and the knife fighter might face an opponent armed with other diverse weapons.

As already stated, the type of guard favored by modern fencers is oriented toward the parry, a defensive movement. It is very dangerous to attempt a fencing parry with a knife, by reason of the weapon's short length and mobility. A two inch misjudgment of distance on the part of the parrier could easily result in a crippling slash to his fingers. Also, a common knife fighting tactic is to feint a thrust, inviting a parry, and then to slash at the parrying hand. At best, the parry is of questionable value in knife combat.

The closest that my knife comes to being used defensively is in a counter-attack, or a *stop hit*. This is an attack made upon the enemy's attack, designed to strike before it does. When genuine defensive action is necessary, evasive footwork is used, along with an accurate yet unconscious awareness of relative distances.

The medieval ideal, which demanded familiarity with many aggression-oriented guards, is well suited to the fight with knives. Logic demands that we accept the value of this theory.

The working definition of "guard" that will be used in this book is flexible and realistic. It is the same medieval definition previously mentioned: "legs, body, hands, and weapon, in readiness to commence action". Generally this is the position of a man and his knife when he is not executing a technique, but is prepared to do so. For instance, if the knife fighter keeps his weapon in a concealed sheath in his front right pants pocket, he is "on guard" every time that he puts his hand into that pocket and touches the handle.

In the world of edged weapons enthusiasts there has been great controversy over which is better in a guard: to have the right leg advanced, or the left. The truth is that there are strengths and weaknesses in both stances.

A left leg leading guard is more aggressive than a right leg leading guard, and gives better balance if the knife is held in the right hand. The combination of a forward lunge on the right leg with a timed slash is very effective when initiated from a guard with the left foot advanced. This covers more distance than the standard lunge, from a right foot leading position. A left leg forward guard makes the upper body settle naturally into an attitude in which the right hand and arm are hard to hit without being exposed to a counter-attack.

A common criticism of this stance is that the right foot leading stance has a reach advantage of about half a foot over it. This is only true if no *shoulder english* is being used in executing the movement. If cutting or thrusting in a left foot forward guard, a small counter-clockwise twist of the shoulders will give a longer reach.

The left leg leading guard nevertheless has its

25

weak points. It leaves the entire left side rather exposed, and the chest faces the opponent squarely, presenting a large target.

The right leg leading guard protects the body by placing it behind the knife-hand, and the natural torsion of the shoulders makes a small target of the upper torso. Yet this type of stance leaves the right arm and weapon-hand quite vulnerable to attack. Guards with the right foot leading are generally better for defensive rather than offensive work.

Both stances are good, yet each is suited for a different use. It is well to become comfortable with both stances, changing from one to the other as demanded by the situation.

Always keep both knees bent. This is vital, for it permits hair-trigger footwork. Even in a lunge, never completely lock the rear leg. When not actually executing a technique, distribute your weight evenly between both feet. Imbalance is fatal, sometimes even when it lasts but an instant.

A deep stance will lower your center of gravity, making the whole guard more stable. In addition it will make protection of the groin and legs easier. The low stance has an obvious value for the large man or woman, who will often leave themselves open while attacking.

The body should be crouched forward slightly, yet relaxed and flexible in hips, waist, back, and shoulders.

Positioning your hands in a ready and useful attitude is also important. It is impossible to cite a single hand position as being superior to all others, but the main thing is to never involuntarily expose your hands and forearms. This mistake is often committed by adopting a guard where the hands are far in front of the body. It is all right to assume such a position for a split-second when the hands are in motion, but it is very dangerous while still looking for an opening with an indecisive spirit.

Never assume a guard with the elbows more than 9 inches from the body. If the distance is over 9 inches, it will expose the hands and forearms to attack. Sometimes a guard is weakened on purpose though; this will be discussed in a following section.

The following guard does not commit its user to any particular technique, so I call it the *conservative guard*.

Take a natural stance, feet parallel and shoulder width apart. Step directly forward with the left leg; the left foot is now advanced one normal pace, or 30 inches. Bend both knees deeply, (a one-third squat), but not overly so, allowing the feet to pivot 45 degrees to the right without changing their relative positions. This movement should lower the body by about 6 inches, perhaps a bit more. Incline the torso slightly forward, and bring both hands up, elbows bent, on a level with the bottom of the rib cage. In this left foot leading stance, the right hand is on a vertical line with the groin, and the left hand is directly over the left thigh. Both forearms are parallel to the ground, the left pointing 45 degrees to the right, the right pointing straight ahead. If an average size man takes this guard, his hands will be 7 to 9 inches apart. This guard bears some similarity to a boxer's, save that the hands are lower, and the knees are far more flexed.

I have described a left foot forward stance. The right foot forward conservative guard is basically the same, except that the knife-hand is over the leading leg.

The conservative guard, whether with right or left foot leading, should be thought of as a home base from which all other guards, offensive, and defensive actions originate.

In this guard, your stance may be narrowed upon demand. The space between the feet could be as little as 6 inches. Such a guard cannot be easily used as a multi-purpose fighting position. The narrow stance is only assumed in preparation for a specific technique, such as a long surprise lunge. A very low stance is useful if the ground is slippery, or if footwork is difficult for some other reason.

If the knife is in the right hand, it can be held behind the right thigh. When combined with the stance of the conservative guard this tactic is very effective against the "wild man" type of opponent, who will often want to move in close, go for body thrusts, and wrestle. This guard modification is excellent when combined with kicking, or when fighting against a fast, skillful, kicker. It puts the weapon-hand out of harm's way.

As a preparation for a powerful backhand slash a *cross-arm guard* can be used. In it, the forearms are loosely crossed in front of the abdomen, close to the body. The knife hand is held under the empty one, protecting it from possible attacks.

A sub-conscious intuition that can be developed only through training is needed to react to any given situation with the proper guard.

Grips

It is now time to turn to the subject of grips. Many ways of holding a knife exist, and all have had proponents at various time and places. Though quite a few grips are considered obsolete by modern knife fighters, the ideal grip has never been found. The reason: there is no such thing. As with methods of carrying knives, and forming guard positions, there is no universal grip that is good for every possible situation. Every grip limits its user to a certain range of actions. For this reason, three grips will be examined. These three, taken collectively, are the best. They allow the fighter proficient in all of them to utilize an extremely wide range of tactics. In studying these three grips, their

GRIPS

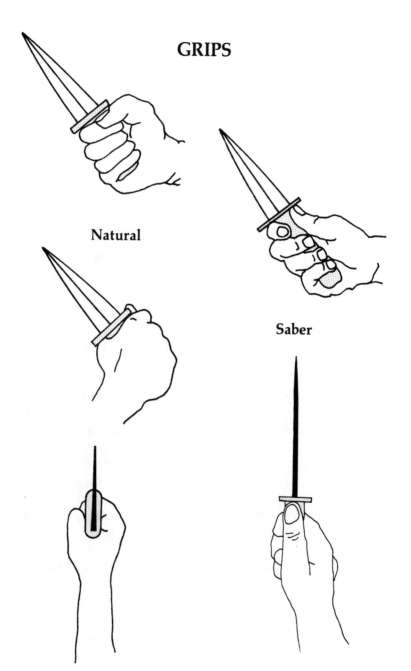

Natural

Saber

weak points will be analyzed no less than their advantages.

The accompanying diagram of standard slashes (or cuts) and thrusts must be referred to in order to understand the following comments. The numbers on it, and in the text, represent seven commonly used cuts/slashes and the standard thrust. Only one thrust is shown in the diagram because no matter where the standard thrust is aimed, it travels in a straight line with much the same bodily movement.

This diagram is not an illustration of targets, but of strike actions. Therefore, do not visualize a human figure at its center. If this is done, for example, cut number one might be thought of as a downward cut at the head. In reality, it would never be so used. Rather, it would probably be delivered to the opponent's knife-hand, arm, or shoulder.

The *saber grip* was popularized by the respected John Styers, of *Cold Steel* fame. A good all-around grip, it is excellent for slashes one, two, three, and five, slightly awkward for four and seven, and poor for cut six. The saber grip is good for long distance thrusting, but it is easy to jam the thumb against the cross-guard when doing so. This grip gives a long reach, by reason of the 45 degree angle of blade and fist.

The second grip is called the *complete grip* by William Cassidy. Occasionally it is referred to as *quarter saber*. It is superb for slash four, good for three and six, slightly awkward for cuts one, two, and five, and poor when used for cut seven. It is a good thrusting grip, yet one must be careful not to loose the knife during withdrawal. Like the saber grip, the complete or quarter saber grip maximizes the knife fighter's reach.

The *natural grip,* also known as the *Hammer, Hatchet,* and *Overhand Grip,* is in current disrepute with knife fighters. However, it is a natural grip

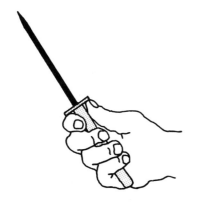

**Complete, or
Quarter Saber**

Ice Pick

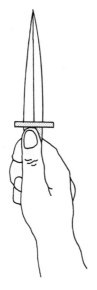

indeed, and so it will be around for as long as men pick up knives. This grip gives a shorter reach than the others, for in it the knife and fist form a 90 degree angle. It is good for cuts one, two, three, and five, slightly awkward for four and seven, and when unmodified, very bad when used for cut six. The natural grip stands supreme when short, powerful thrusts are called for.

If the above paragraphs have shown us anything, it is that any given grip is good for certain things, yet bad for others. Because of this, I advocate changing from one grip to another during a fight. Many experts will deride my suggested approach here. Granted that this is a very unorthodox technique, yet I believe it is an extremely practical and useful one. It permits the employment of a wider range of tactics than any single grip possibly can.

The key to this technique is to keep a non-committal grip on the knife when not actually cutting, thrusting, or feinting. The word non-committal does not signify a particular grip; it could be any grip at all. It refers to a slight floating feeling in the hand, prior to the initiation of any specific action. The knife must **not** be held in a loose, sloppy manner, or it will fly from the hand with any small movement. I suggest that this feeling involves more mental than physical preparation.

When changing grips, the forearm must not shift position. A tiny gesture of the hand, and one, perhaps two fingers, is sufficient. Then, when striking, tighten the new grip as your hand goes into the motion. After recovery, hold your knife in the non-committal grip again.

Obviously, changing grips in this manner is not for everyone. Chances are that someone adept at changing grips may not even call upon this talent in a heated knife fight. So if you have not seriously practiced grip changing for a minimum of a few hundred hours, don't try it. It is included here only for the would-be expert, who wishes to extend his talents and fighting options beyond that of the average reader.

To be useful in combat, there must be no conscious decision involved in grip changing. A target is choosen, the right strike action is decided upon, the best grip for it taken, and the cut or thrust is executed; all of this occurs in a split-second, on a sub-conscious level. This aspect of grip changing is hard to master. But after 500 training bouts or more, the series of mental and physical actions involved becomes automatic. At this point, the series is a series no longer, but a one-step process.

The following is a realistic series of movements demonstrating the principles set forth above.

Fighters "A" and "B" are in conservative guard positions. Three paces separate them. Both hold their knives in the saber grip.

"A" closes the gap, putting himself within "B's" reach, and allows "B" to make the first move. "B" cuts at "A's" hand. "A" jerks his hand out of the way. "B" draws his arm back to re-assume a proper guard, but "A" follows it in with his own, and slashes "B's" forearm. Not powerfully enough, though. "B" lunges, right leg leading, attempting to score a chest thrust. "A" sidesteps to "B's" left, (the empty, or weaponless side), changes to the complete grip, and delivers a heavy cut to the back of "B's" left knee. "A" then steps forward and turns, so that he is facing "B's" left side, out of range. "B" tries to correct this by adjusting his stance, attempting to make a quarter-turn to his left. As "B" does this, he realizes that he is hurt, and looses his mental balance.

Now both fighters are "squared off" again. "A" moves in, changing to the natural grip. When he is at the proper distance, he exposes his right hand to a cut from "B". "B" takes the bait, and slashes. "A" slips his right hand from the path of the cut, traps "B's" wrist with his left hand, and sees an opening. "A" then performs the final movement, a hard thrust to "B's" throat.

Cuts and Slashes

The cut is the strike most often used in knife fighting. There are three types of cuts: the *power slash*, the *snap-cut*, and the *hook-cut*.

The power slash is a forceful blow; the shoulder and back muscles are fully employed in its delivery. Nevertheless, it should not be a wild, round-house swing of the arm. It is a somewhat large movement, but with careful control this cut can be performed in surprisingly little space. The power is developed through the muscle groups utilized, not by the blade's momentum or centrifugal force. It is unwise to use the power slash in an exploratory manner to find the enemy's weak points. If such tactics are called for, it is better to use the snap-cut.

The snap-cut involves a different body motion, resembling strongly the darting of a cat's paw. In it, the hand punches straight toward the target, wrist cocked back. When about an inch over the area to be cut, the knife is snapped down at the target while the extended hand is simultaneously drawn sharply back. This rakes the blade across the target. The snap-cut is nowhere near as forceful a technique as the power slash, but if properly executed it is a quick one, so quick that an effective stop cut, or counter-attack can rarely be launched against it. The main use of the snap-cut is on the enemy's hands, for on them are located vital tendons that are relatively unprotected by surrounding tissue. As it happens, the hands are such mobile targets that it is often difficult to hit them except with a snap-cut.

The punching motion which initiates this cut is

DIAGRAM OF SEVEN CUTS & THE STANDARD THRUST

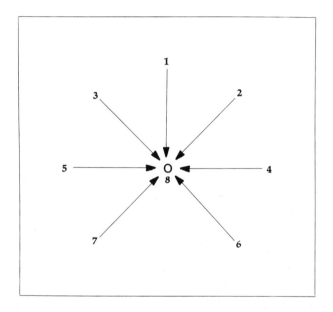

This diagram is not an illustration of targets, but of strike actions. Therefore, do not visualize a human figure at its center. If this is done, for example, cut number one might be thought of as a downward cut at the head. In reality, it would never be so used. Rather, it would probably be delivered to the opponent's knife-hand, arm, or shoulder.

not part of the cut itself, but is a preparation for it. The punch does not give power to the cut, it merely brings the knife to the place where the actual slash can be made. It is a waste of effort to punch hard; speed is paramount here. In the snap-cut, force is generated in the forearm, transmitted to the hand, and then is manifested in the downward snap of the cocked wrist and the whipping back of the extended arm. If done well, the feeling is like that of cracking a whip. This cut is particularly valuable when used against an opponent who is skilled, fast, and excellent at defensive maneuvers. The saber grip lends itself well to this type of cut.

Perhaps I have given the impression that power slashes are always strong, and snap-cuts are always relatively weak. This is not wholly true, for one man's snap-cut may be as forceful as another's power slash. Yet everyone has room for improvement, and both should be practiced to gain speed and power.

Finally, the hook-cut. Here the knife is aimed at a point 3 inches to the right of the target, (if the knife is held in the right hand). The knife is angled lengthwise behind the target. When in this position, the wrist is bent and the blade is laid against the rear of the area to be cut, and then is ripped through it left to right, the attacker drawing the knife back towards himself. The quarter-saber or complete grip must be used, because this cut is nearly impossible with any other. The hook-cut has a limited number of applications, but what it does, it does well. (See illustrations: Bleeders and Immobilizers.)

Thrusts

There are three kinds of thrusts: the *snap-thrust, standard thrust,* and the *hook-thrust.*

In the snap-thrust the knife is jabbed at the target, quickly and lightly. Without a pause, and even faster, the extended hand is then withdrawn. Power and deep penetration are not the objectives of this attack. If it hits, a one or two inch deep wound will be the result. There is no movement of the torso during the snap-thrust, and no follow through.

Snap-thrusts are mainly used to gain a psychological advantage by disorienting the enemy, or shaking his confidence. Basically a probing technique used to feel out the adversary's defenses, it can be fatal if placed properly. Though by no means a power tactic, the snap-thrust can be delivered with great accuracy

In the standard thrust the knife travels in a straight line to the target. It is delivered as forcefully as possible to insure deep penetration. Power is critical, for it is difficult to pierce a full half-foot of flesh. Strength is generated by a small twist of the hips, and is transferred through the shoulder to the arm. The shoulder must not be tensed, for this inhibits the natural flow of speed and power. Unlike the snap-thrust, the standard thrust is performed with a follow through of the shoulders, which would be a counter-clockwise twist if the thrust was done with the right arm. The knife hand must then be drawn back to its original position, which depends upon the guard that is being used.

The hook-thrust is exactly like the well known boxer's hook-punch in terms of body movement. However, the hook-thrust is virtually unknown to both the Oriental and Occidental schools of knife fighting. Prudence must be exercised in utilizing this strike, for it leaves the entire body wide open. Nevertheless, it does have some interesting applications. For example, a man well schooled in self defense will often try to nullify a thrust with a simple forearm block. This would be ineffectual against a hook-thrust though, and the "expert" would be skewered anyway. This thrust can also be used against an opponent with a strong frontal defense. By flashing the knife to his right, the attacker draws his opponent's attention to that quarter. Immediately following this diversion, the true strike is made: a hook-thrust to the opponent's left side below his ribs. Coming from the side, this attack would bypass both of the defender's hands. As with all cuts and thrusts, upon completion the extended arm must be swiftly yanked out of the enemy's reach.

The hook-thrust is powerful, but it has its drawbacks. One of them has already been mentioned; another is that it can be utilized only at close range.

The blade angle of the natural grip is perfect for this thrust. Power is developed the same way as in the standard thrust, but additional force can be gained by slightly hunching the back and raising the shoulders.

In all three thrusts, the grip must be tightened firmly at penetration and recovery. It is easy to lose hold of the handle during a hard thrust, particularly if it is slippery with blood.

At this point, a few words about the relationship between cutting and thrusting are in order.

At least one rhythm is naturally formed in every fight. Thrusting tends to break the rhythm present at the time, while cutting tends to preserve it. Knowledge of this can be capitalized upon, for there are times when the knife fighter will wish to change the fight's rhythm. At other times, he may wish to preserve the unchanged rhythm.

Thrusts are harder to combine with other offensive movements than cuts, but can be meshed with patterns of footwork somewhat more easily. A feinting thrust is generally more fluid than a feinting cut, yet it is more vulnerable to counter attack, as are all thrusts. For this reason, use the standard and hook thrusts only if the opponent leaves a clear opening, or if his knife-wrist is gripped.

As a rule, thrusts are applied to the torso, and cuts are used to attack the limbs. See the section on targets, and the accompanying illustrations.

Anatomical Considerations

To apply a cut or thrust to the proper target, it is necessary to have a practical knowledge of human anatomy. Correct placement is imperative, for without it even the perfect strike may come to naught.

An effectual knife wound will fall into one of three categories. It will be a bleeder, an immobilizer, or will be the type that kills swiftly.

Bleeder wounds result from the severing of an artery. Rarely putting an enemy immediately out of action, they are often fatal if unattended. There are several arteries, though, that if severed will cause death in less than a minute.

The true bleeder is nearly always caused by a slash, for an artery is very hard to sever with a thrust. The blood vessel can literally squirm to one side of the point when pressure is put on the tissue above it. Yet some arteries lie too deep for most slashes; the femoral artery and the aorta for example. Another is the sub-clavian artery, which has protecting bone structures on all sides. These are to be stabbed.

The main problem with bleeders follows. Imagine that you have just neatly slashed the brachial artery of your opponent. His shirt sleeve has a wide cut in it, and you can see the blood spurting out. Very good. Now for the problem. Some people will look down at their own blood, forget about their enemy, and faint. Others will have common sense, and run away. Then there are those who will think, "It's him or me!" and respond with violent aggression. Still others will be so adrenalized, drugged, or insane, that they won't immediately notice the blood and pain, or if they do they might not even care.

TARGETS: BLEEDERS

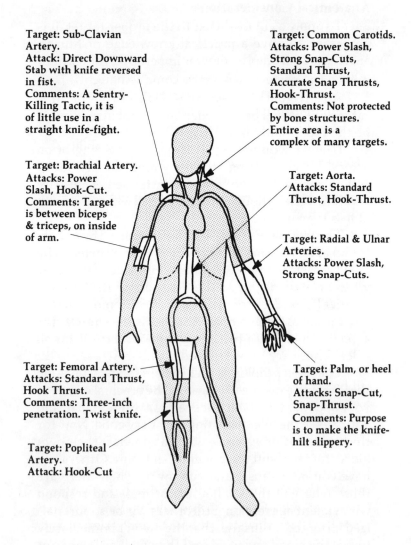

Target: Sub-Clavian Artery.
Attack: Direct Downward Stab with knife reversed in fist.
Comments: A Sentry-Killing Tactic, it is of little use in a straight knife-fight.

Target: Brachial Artery.
Attacks: Power Slash, Hook-Cut.
Comments: Target is between biceps & triceps, on inside of arm.

Target: Common Carotids.
Attacks: Power Slash, Strong Snap-Cuts, Standard Thrust, Accurate Snap Thrusts, Hook-Thrust.
Comments: Not protected by bone structures. Entire area is a complex of many targets.

Target: Aorta.
Attacks: Standard Thrust, Hook-Thrust.

Target: Radial & Ulnar Arteries.
Attacks: Power Slash, Strong Snap-Cuts.

Target: Femoral Artery.
Attacks: Standard Thrust, Hook Thrust.
Comments: Three-inch penetration. Twist knife.

Target: Palm, or heel of hand.
Attacks: Snap-Cut, Snap-Thrust.
Comments: Purpose is to make the knife-hilt slippery.

Target: Popliteal Artery.
Attack: Hook-Cut

Never count on a bleeder being the *coup de grace*. Always remain cautious and ready to begin further action. Never rely on different subjects responding to the same wound with the same psychological reaction. Do not make hasty and dangerous assumptions. Sometimes a superficial cut will bleed a great deal at first but will clot after a few minutes.

A good bleeder is a major wound, but the knife fighter must not allow himself the feeling of security after delivering one to his adversary.

Immobilizing wounds are dealt to specific muscle and tendon complexes. Their purpose is to eliminate or weaken the mechanical balance, or functionability, of part of the enemy's body, generally a limb. The immediate object of all immobilizing attacks is to cut the target area to the bone, rendering the muscle group as non-functional. A thrust cannot do this, so the immobilizing injury is usually brought about by a power slash. When cutting, the knife blade must always be at a right angle to the target. Here pin-point accuracy is less important than great force. Still, a one inch misplacement can make an attack ineffectual.

As with bleeders, snap judgments and overconfidence here are dangerous and undesirable. Wait a few seconds until the enemy tries to use the stricken limb that your slash may have immobilized. Then there will be no need for assumptions; you will know the result of your attack, and what to do next.

Those wounds that cause death in ten seconds or less are called quick kills. Other strikes may be fatal in ten seconds to a minute, but these do not do the job fast enough to be covered here. They leave the injured party time to thrash about, and perhaps make a dying counter-attack. These slower kills include stabbed femoral arteries, thrusts to the aorta, and various other forms of gross tissue damage. Note that the above two

TARGETS: IMMOBILIZERS

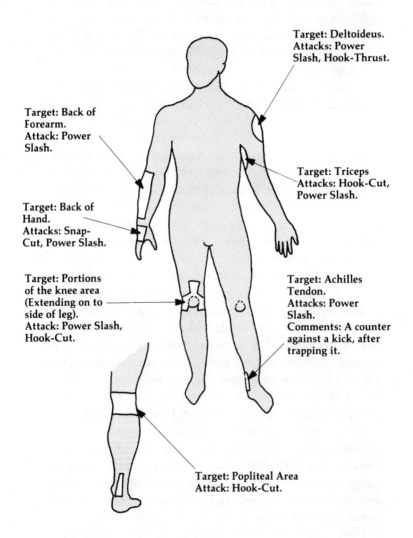

Target: Deltoideus.
Attacks: Power
Slash, Hook-Thrust.

Target: Back of
Forearm.
Attack: Power
Slash.

Target: Triceps
Attacks: Hook-Cut,
Power Slash.

Target: Back of
Hand.
Attacks: Snap-
Cut, Power Slash.

Target: Portions
of the knee area
(Extending on to
side of leg).
Attack: Power Slash,
Hook-Cut.

Target: Achilles
Tendon.
Attacks: Power
Slash.
Comments: A counter
against a kick, after
trapping it.

Target: Popliteal Area
Attack: Hook-Cut.

were designated as bleeders, even though in time they would prove fatal.

In face-to-face combat, quick kill wounds are best inflicted when the adversary has already been badly hurt by bleeder and/or immobilizer attacks. The reason: all quick kill attacks involve coming very close to the enemy. All of the quick kills targets are located on the head and torso, none on the limbs. When executing a quick kill strike, it is best to pump the knife handle a few times to enlarge the wound. This means that your body will be well within the enemy's knife-reach. If the opponent is able to use his weapon at this point, an error in the execution of the attack might be fatal to the attacker.

Most of the quick kill targets are partially protected by bone. Some are covered by it. The quick kill strike must be very accurate, as well as extremely powerful.

A final word about quick kills. If the opponent has fallen, great care must be taken when finishing him off. An example follows.

The enemy has been disarmed by a forceful cut that flung the knife from his hand, rendering his arm useless for fighting. One of his legs is crippled, and bleeding heavily. He is kneeling on the ground, still conscious. Assuming that total neutralization is necessary, the next reasonable step would be to launch a quick kill attack. Yet even though it is impossible for the opponent to fight, he can still thrash about on the ground, grapple with his enemy, ward off the finishing strike with his remaining good arm, and generally make a sloppy scene. This may not matter to a 250 pounder who has just dropped a puny adversary. But this same untidy situation can be very dangerous to the attacker when the downed opponent has a considerable size advantage over him.

At this point, the wounded man should be held

TARGETS: QUICK KILLS

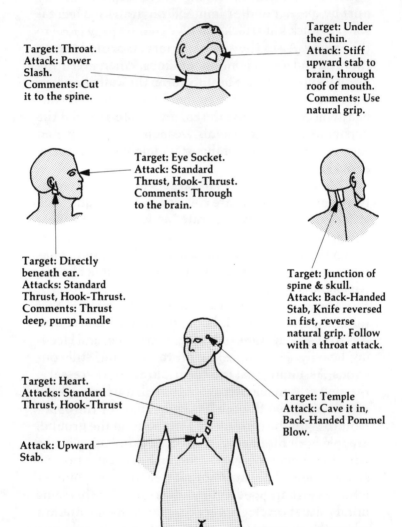

Target: Throat.
Attack: Power Slash.
Comments: Cut it to the spine.

Target: Under the chin.
Attack: Stiff upward stab to brain, through roof of mouth.
Comments: Use natural grip.

Target: Eye Socket.
Attack: Standard Thrust, Hook-Thrust.
Comments: Through to the brain.

Target: Directly beneath ear.
Attacks: Standard Thrust, Hook-Thrust.
Comments: Thrust deep, pump handle

Target: Junction of spine & skull.
Attack: Back-Handed Stab, Knife reversed in fist, reverse natural grip. Follow with a throat attack.

Target: Heart.
Attacks: Standard Thrust, Hook-Thrust

Attack: Upward Stab.

Target: Temple
Attack: Cave it in, Back-Handed Pommel Blow.

motionless in order to administer the final strike. But this is a good tactic only if the strike will not cause heavy bleeding. For example, if he administers a throat slash, the killer's face and upper body may be immediately covered with blood. "High profile" indeed. Of course this is to be avoided as a general principle.

As an alternative, the old adage about skinning cats comes to mind. Here one would stay out of the wounded man's reach, and kill him with a few powerful kicks to the head.

I am not saying that the quick killing strike is a defective tactic. All that the above recommends is that the knife fighter must remain flexible in thought, and precise in deed; even to the very end.

Footwork

Now we come to footwork. As stated, footwork is the primary means of defense when knife fighting. While this is true, footwork is closely related to offensive action as well. Because of its pervasive nature, footwork is in a very real sense the vital foundation of this art. Any fighting-style that is based upon impractical footwork is like a house built on sand.

European fencers use but a single pattern of footwork; a straight forward-and-backward shuffle, never allowing the left foot to lead. The various oriental martial arts possess many kinds of footwork, each either associated with a particular stance, or forming a certain geometric pattern. Of these two, the oriental style is the most valuable, but there is a third alternative.

I favor natural footwork. This entails not worrying very much about form or style, and simply maintaining a natural, logical approach. For instance, if in a right foot forward stance, step with the left. With the left foot forward, step with the right. Sometimes position is changed without switching the leading foot, like a fencer does, but only for a short distance. The opponent can be approached by sideways-stepping like a crab, as well. It is possible to cover ground astonishingly fast in this unlikely way. However, crab-stepping should only be done in short bursts. And never let your body bob up and down when crab-stepping.

Any footwork requires that both knees must always be flexed; never lock one of your legs. It is good to keep your weight slightly forward, on the balls of your feet. The motion of stepping is generated in the hips, not in the muscles of the legs.

It is psychologically advantageous to strongly take the initiative at the beginning of the knife fight. If probing tactics rather than a vigorous initial attack are in order, seize the initiative by using footwork to unsettle your opponent.

It is bad to yield much ground suddenly, unless it is a deceptive tactic used to set the enemy up for something. On the whole, though, sidestepping is better than retreat.

When combined with a step forward on the right foot (initiated in a left foot forward stance), some right-handed strikes gain tremendous power; notably the hook thrust, power slash, and standard thrust. If the weapon is held in the left hand, the step is with the left foot.

Front snap-kicks aimed at the enemy's knife-hand and groin can produce telling effects. Front and side thrust or power kicks can be directed to his knees. But be cautious when employing kicks. If the extended leg is trapped, the kicker is done for. A kicking attack is best applied in the wake of a hand-feint. All kicks must be low, swift, and powerful.

Forearm blocks are used only to counter a very limited number of blows, such as direct downward cuts at the head. A block induces the adversary to pull his knife back a few inches, thus cutting the blocking arm or hand. This can easily happen, for the knife is a very mobile weapon.

Grappling

Grappling, that is, grasping the opponent's knife-wrist is an excellent tactic. The wrist is seized when it first moves, or while still in a guard position. Grappling is too risky when the arm is fully in motion. Momentum could actually break the thumb of the grappling hand.

In this technique the wrist is not really grabbed, but is trapped. The wrist itself need not be gripped as tightly as you think. The idea is to encircle the opponent's wrist with your index finger, middle finger, and thumb. Then tighten your fingers into a bracelet about the wrist, using the tendons of your hand and forearm to hold them together, not your chest muscles. This kind of *hand-cuff grip* can fit about the wrist loosely, so long as the subject cannot slip his fist through it. When the grip is secure the chest and biceps are still relaxed. If the enemy tries to free his arm, his movements are controlled only by the power of the grappler's shoulder muscle. But he should not be given time to struggle. The grip ought to be followed instantly by a heavy slash to the opponent's trapped arm, or a low thrust to his body. Always sidestep as you grip to protect yourself from a groin kick.

When dealing with an opponent in a very confined place, grappling and thrusting are in order. Footwork and cutting will probably have to be discarded as virtually useless. With an unarmed opponent forget about hand and arm cuts, which are disarming tactics. Thrusting, blocking/grappling, and kicking attacks should be utilized.

Flexibility And Deception

Earlier it was said that the knife fighter must have a flexible mind. The advantages of mental flexibility are presented in the following brief study of deceptive movements, to which this flexibility is closely related.

The purpose of all such tactics is to literally disorient the adversary's mind and body.

Of all deceptive movements, the simple feint is the most elementary. Feints are used to make the enemy move his knife-hand, exposing his forearm and body. They may also force him into bad terrain, or set him up for kicking or grappling. Snap-cuts and snap-thrusts are safest to use as feints. The heavier strikes commit their user to the movement excessively for this purpose.

An efficient feint can be performed with the empty hand. It is flashed in front of the opponent's face at the same moment the true strike is initiated with the weapon-hand. A very confusing move, to say the least.

A similar tactic involves leaving your guard open. In this type of deceptive movement, your guard position is intentionally weak in one area. The enemy sees the opening, and makes a predictable attack. Then, since his course of action was already known before he moved, the enemy's own attack is used against him.

For example, covered in the section on guards is the crossed-arm position. Here the knife-arm is held under the empty one to protect it from attack. In the false, or deceptive variation of this guard the weapon-arm is on top, inviting a backhand slash. As a preparation, move to the outside of the opponent's weapon-arm, just within his knife range. When he takes the bait and initiates a backhand slash, he will expose his own forearm to attack. Now "beat him to the punch" with a stop-hit. This move is called *Backhand Invitation-Backhand Reprisal*.

Positioning the knife behind the right thigh (if the knife is in the right hand) is good when fighting the "wild man" type, but it has another use. When combined with kicking and fast footwork this guard will often make even the experienced adversary temporarily forget about the knife. A fatal mistake on his part, if you do your job right.

Distraction can be produced by waving a jacket at your opponent while concealing your knife. Strike at him rapidly and lightly with the jacket while staying out of reach. Whether he wills it or not, his attention will be momentarily focused on the visible moving object. Do not be surprised when he wastes energy by trying to slash or block the jacket. Strike for the opening that this motion will cause.

In the section on grips, I presented the highly flexible non-committal grip. Certain reasons for its use were given there; yet another will be related now. A non-committal grip allows one to slip the knife from one hand to the other. I am not speaking of the movement that young hoodlums are pictured doing in the movies, (i.e., while far away from the opponent tossing the knife back and forth from hand to hand). Such antics have no purpose. By changing hands I mean a fast, simple movement; switching the knife from right to left, or vice versa. As a preparation for the change, the left hand is brought slightly closer to the right and a bit above it. Above, not below, thus shielding the gesture from the enemy's sight. Notice that in the conservative guard the hands were rather close to begin with, only 7 to 9 inches apart.

Typically, switching is used in the following way. In a right foot forward stance, with knife in his right hand, the fighter faces his adversary. Next the fighter allows the adversary to attack his right arm or hand. The fighter simultaneously switches the knife to his left hand. Stepping forward with his left leg, he slashes the opponent's knife arm, or thrusts to his body. The natural body torsion caused by this maneuver automatically removes the fighter's right arm and hand from the initial attack. *Suggested for advanced students only!*

The self-defense expert who is conditioned to respond to knife attacks with arm holds, locks, and throws is in for a nasty surprise when against a man who has mastered this technique. If one is truly proficient at changing hands it does not matter if one arm is held motionless; there is always a ready spare.

In practice, try to become accustomed to fighting with the knife in your weak hand. Ambidexterity is a valuable skill.

There is another class of deceptive movement that is associated with assassination, and yet another that has to do with sentry killing. Both lie outside the scope of this work, which deals only with face-to-face knife combat.

I have merely indicated here the diverse nature of deceptive movement, and some of the possibilities therein. The subject has much room for further development, and it will please me greatly if my readers invent their own original techniques of deception.

The "TWYFOLD MYND"

At all times, flexibility is imperative to the successful knife fighter. When pressing forward, be ready to commence evasive action. When thrusting, be prepared to change the strike to a cut, or pull the hand back suddenly and completely. The guard, stance, and grip that were proper a moment ago might be all wrong for the new, ever fluctuating situation. Flexibility was called the "Twyfold Mynd" (Twofold Mind) by George Silver.

Genuine flexibility of fighting technique can only be done by reflex, with a total absence of thought. This is a real state of mind in which the knife fighter does not feel fear, confusion, or indecision. Absence of thought is achieved through long training. There is no way to force the development of this state of mind; but when achieved, it will considerably improve your fighting ability.

The system that is outlined in *Slash and Thrust* may be considered an analytical one. While this may be true, I suggest that similar texts are also analytical in nature. Yet my book is analytical only until the reader begins training in earnest, according to the program and advice I have presented. Then the analytical becomes the tangible; and the mere reader the competent student.

IV. Suggestions For Further Study

I have quoted George Silver several times in this text. These citations were from his *Paradoxes of Defence*, a work originally published in 1599. The *Paradoxes* were re-printed in 1933 by the Oxford University Press for the Shakespeare Association.

Paradoxes of Defence contains much common sense and deep thought. It deals with sword combat, yet many of Silver's opinions are valid for the fight with knives as well.

Miyamoto Musashi, who lived from 1584 to 1645, is called "Sword-Saint" by the Japanese. Many men tried to kill Musashi, by drawing weapons against him. Perhaps it is right to regard them as suicides.

In the last year of his life he wrote *Go Rin No Sho*, or *A Book of Five Rings*. This book deals with the use of the two-handed Japanese sword, but surprisingly, a majority of its content can be related directly to knife fighting. *A Book of Five Rings* deserves extensive study.

An English translation is published by the Overlook Press of Woodstock, New York.

Of the modern books on knife combat, I recommend *The Complete Book of Knife Fighting*, by William

Cassidy. Cassidy's rationale is often at variance with mine, but this makes the book all the more valuable. It gives insight into a different method. *The Complete Book of Knife· Fighting* is published by Paladin Press at Boulder, Colorado.

Other suggested titles from Paladin Press are: *Cold Steel*, by John Styers; and *Get Tough*, by Capt. W. E. Fairbairn. These two books are classic reprints, and were originally published around 1940.

Appendix: Throwing Concealable Edged Weapons

Knife throwing is a controversial subject. In the words of one knife-fighting expert: "The chances are excellent that you will miss, alarm and quite possibly arm" an opponent. There may be times however, when knife throwing can be applied as a favorable tactic. There are also various edged weapons expressly designed to be thrown: cloth darts, shuriken, sharpened coins, etc. The following methods cover both conventional edged weapons and those meant to be thrown.

EUROPEAN METHODS

The Underhand Straight Throw

The conventional knife is held in the palm, clamped there by the thumb alone. Either the knife point or the pommel is nearly level with the fingertips, not projecting more than 1½ inches beyond them. With the exception of the thumb, the fingers are straight and relaxed. The arm is relaxed, hanging naturally at the side of the body. The knife is thrown by swinging the arm up and forward, keeping the elbow rather stiff. It is released just before the arm

EDGED THROWING WEAPONS

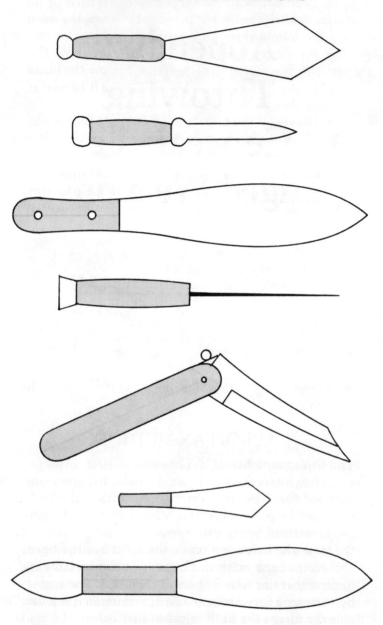

European

becomes on line with the target. There is little or no wrist action; the knife is allowed to slip from the open hand. No follow-through is required.

If the target is less than 5 feet away, hold the knife with the *point* at the fingertips. Throw the blade straight into the target, without allowing it to spin at all in the air.

However, if the target is more than 5 feet away, hold the knife with the *handle* at the fingertips. The object is to give the knife just enough spin to make a half turn in the air, striking the target point first. The knife must always make a precise half turn, no matter what the distance. Obviously less spin is needed to give the knife a half turn at 20 feet than at 10.

The underhand Straight Throw has one outstanding peculiarity: it seems to work best with those knives that are not made for throwing. For example, this throw was traditionally used with the Spanish lockblade *Cuchillo,* which is a large folding knife. While applicable to a wide variety of blades, the underhand straight throw is ideally suited to heavy-handled knives of modest length.

In this style of throwing, any misjudgment of distance up to 1½ feet is acceptable. This means that if you estimate the distance to a target as 12 feet, and threw accordingly, the actual distance can be as much as 13½ feet, or as little as 10½ feet. The chances are good that the knife will go in point first anyway. Individual nuances will shrink or increase this margin of acceptable error.

The Overhand Spinning Throw

Here the throwing arm is raised above the head with elbow bent, with the knife held comfortably in the first three or four fingers of the hand. The arm is then snapped forward and down, and when it is level with the target the knife is released.

While mechanically the simplest of throws, an examination of its theory and practice proves it to be the most complex.

The knife can be gripped by blade or handle. If gripped by the blade, it will have to rotate ½, 1½, or 2½ times in midair to strike the target point first. If gripped by the handle, it will have to spin 0, 1, or 2 times. When the overhand spinning throw is used, the knife will commonly make a half turn in 4 feet, 1 in 8 feet, 1½ in 12, and so on. Blind luck would have the point hit the target once out of every eight tries. To substantially better these odds three measures must be taken. The distance to the target must be closed or widened until it approximates a distance in which the knife will make a given number of turns. Then the proper grip for this number of turns is taken on the knife. Finally the knife is thrown. It is vital that every throw gives exactly the same rate of spin to the blade. If the rate of spin varies from throw to throw, there is no way to judge how many revolutions the knife will make in a given distance.

Circus knife throwers always use the overhand spinning throw, for it allows power to be used, and with great accuracy. Yet target throwing is very different from combat throwing. The professional can take time to wipe his sweaty hands on a dry cloth. A damp hand will give a different spin to the blade than a dry one, making the throw unsure. He will invariably use a knife made expressly for throwing, having no sharp edges. It is very possible to cut one's hand when throwing a sharp knife by the blade, using the overhand spinning throw. The professional does not throw under unusual stress, and can choose his target's distance. Stress will make the rate of spin vary from throw to throw, nullifying all attempts to equate a given distance with a fixed number of spins. Furthermore, stage knife throwers seldom work with moving targets. When they do, it always moves at a fixed speed and in a predetermined pattern. Clearly, the circus knife thrower has control over the targets he will engage, and the circumstances under which he will do so. The combat thrower cannot count on being presented with such favorable options.

In the overhead spinning throw any misjudgment of distance over 4 to 8 inches will make the strike ineffectual. This margin of acceptable error is small because the throw gives a fast rate of spin to the knife.

This style of throwing can be put to good use on a target that is totally unaware of the knife thrower. Yet as will be seen, there are many superior alternatives.

CHINESE METHODS

The Cloth Dart

Short strips of cloth are tied to the tang of a small blade, which is either cylindrical in cross-section, or resembles a dagger. Cloth darts are thrown much like an ordinary dart, save that there is a strong follow-through. They can also be thrown sidearm, or can be palmed and thrown backhand. Whatever technique is used, the cloth dart must be thrown very fast. If thrown slowly, the cloth tail will not stabilize the dart's flight.

These darts are often seen with shallow grooves running the length of the blade. The purpose of the grooves was to retain a poisonous herbal compound, of the consistency of soft tar.

Targets of the unpoisoned cloth dart are the forehead, temples, eyes, and throat. The cloth dart is seldom heavy enough to achieve a fatal torso penetration. A large blade needs a piece of cloth the size of a

EDGED THROWING WEAPONS

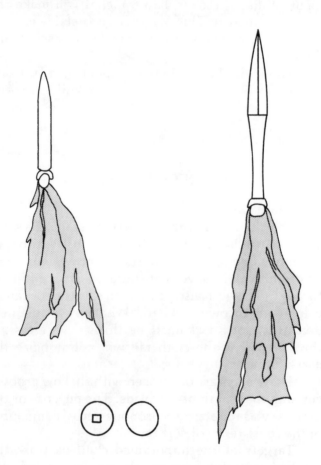

Chinese

pocket handkerchief. The cloth puts considerable drag on the flying weapon, as well as making a distinct flapping sound as it travels through the air.

Sharpened Coins

These are the size of a half-dollar; razor sharp through all 360 degrees. Sharpened coins seem to work best when thrown in a sidearm fashion, but can also be thrown backhand and overhand. They are held between the tip of the thumb and the side of the index finger.

Traditional targets are somewhat limited; the temple, eyes, and throat. Obviously accuracy is important. Power is also a problem, for the coins are rather light. However, Chinese coin throwers did not concern themslves with these fine points. At close range and without taking exact aim, they would throw six or so coins at once in a single flurry at the face of their opponents. Fatal penetrations were not the aim of this. The objective was to break the enemy's attack, distracting him, then closing the distance so that the attacker's main weapon could be employed.

JAPANESE METHODS

Shuriken

Generally these are sharpened steel rods, $\frac{1}{4}$ to $\frac{3}{8}$ inch in diameter, and from 4 to 8 inches long. They are always worn concealed. In modern society shuriken are occasionally disguised as pens and pencils, painted an appropriate color, and even equipped with a pocket clip.

The Japanese method of throwing the shuriken is as follows. Hold the weapon as in the underhand straight throw. The throwing arm is lifted high, with wrist perfectly straight, elbow nearly so. Then the

EDGED THROWING WEAPONS

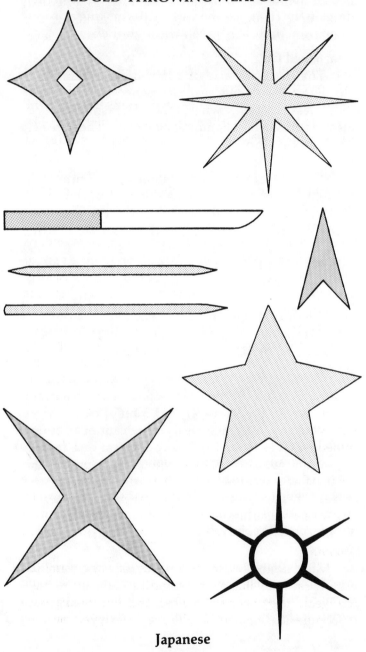

Japanese

62

arm is swung down towards the target, wrist stiff, elbow now straightened. Allow the shuriken to slip from your palm just before your arm becomes level with the target. There is no follow-through.

Theoretically, this throw is basically the same as the overthrow spinning throw. A given distance is equated with the number of revolutions the knife will describe in mid-air when thrown that distance. The weapon is grasped with the butt at the fingertips, or the point, depending on whether it will make an even number of complete spins, or a number of spins and one additional half spin. Sharpening both ends of the shuriken will make the last step unnecessary.

But the Japanese method of throwing shuriken possesses a significant advantage over the standard overhand spinning knife throw. The knife's rate of turn is twice as slow in the Japanese method, thus the margin of acceptable distance misjudgment is doubled, (8–16 inches compared with 4–8 inches). This is an advantage in a close combat situation, where a moving target is the rule, not the exception.

The Japanese style of throwing shuriken is inapplicable to large fighting knives with fingerguards. It is not an instinctive method, which is an important factor when the thrower is under stress. When throwing at a target whose distance cannot be determined (such as when turning to the rear and throwing simultaneously) the odds are one to four that the point of the weapon will effectively penetrate the target. These odds are for double pointed shuriken. If only one end is sharpened, they are one to eight.

Shaken

Most edged weapons enthusiasts are familiar with these star-shaped instruments. During the past few years they have enjoyed an amazing resurgence in popularity. Shaken are properly gripped by one point, using the thumb and the side of the index finger. They are thrown overhand, sidearm, and backhanded. Whatever throwing technique is used, a powerful spin should be put on the shaken by a snap of the wrist. This is not to make the shaken cut a swath through the target, as has been suggested by some pseudo-experts. Rather it serves to increase accuracy, as the rifling does in a gun. Very few shaken are made to deliver a slashing strike, and these are of inefficient design.

Shaken are easy to conceal, but hard to draw. They tend to snag in clothing. In order to gain sufficient penetration for a lethal torso strike (four inches or more), the overall size of a five-pointed shaken would have to be at least ten inches in diameter. With more than five points, it would have to be even larger. Shaken this size would obviously be cumbersome and impractical.

Because of their design limitations, shaken are classed by the Japanese as distracting nuisance weapons not lethal ones. They are simply used to create an opening for the thrower, as with sharpened coins.

Summary

For true practical efficiency, the hand-thrown concealable edged weapon must possess two characteristics. First, its flight must be tactically stable, i.e., one must be reasonably certain that its point or blade will hit the target regardless of chance variables. Second, the weapon's design should enable it to penetrate the target to the depth of four inches, preferably more.

All of the techniques discussed so far can be useful in a combat situation, but none gives the weapon the true stability we associate with an arrow in flight. Cloth darts limit target penetration by their light weight; shaken by their design characteristics. Chinese oral tradition states that it is possible to deliver dependable, deeply penetrating strikes with sharpened coins, but also notes that such a capability comes after years of intensive practice, and then only to those with an individual genius for the weapon.

OTHER METHODS

The Chakram
A weapon of Northern India, the chakram should be thought of as a flying axe that always hits with the edge. Chakra are sharpened to a knife-edge around their entire perimeter. They can deliver a penetrating cut to muscle, and their effect on bone is that of a heavy cleaver. The chakram is held between thumb and index finger, and thrown backhand, sidearm, and overhand. Targets are the head, throat, junction of spine and skull, spine, and when thrown vertically, the breast-bone and groin. Reliable sources state that the chakram's effective range exceeds 90 feet. This may seem incredible at first, but one should consider that the distance record for throwing a 4½ pound discus is 232 feet 6 inches.

The Hand Quarrel, Or Irish Dart
In the first centuries of the Christian era, the hand quarrel was strongly associated with the Irish, hence one of its many names. Somewhat later it was used by the barbarian auxiliaries, then the barbarian troops of the declining Roman Army. There is evidence that the medieval mercenaries of Northern Europe were familiar with this instrument.

Held like an ordinary dart, but thrown as a spear, the hand quarrel's flight is stabilized by dart vanes. It is effective as far as it can be thrown, which is very far indeed. Naturally accuracy is important, but the weapon's design allows a precise strike, and the throwing motion is instinctive and unforced. Furthermore, difficult long-range head shots are not mandatory. The weight and shape of the hand quarrel allow it to deliver fatal torso penetrations.

The handle and blade of the modern hand quarrel need not be of any outlandish or impractical shape. With the vanes detached and carried separately the weapon doubles as a servicable guardless boot knife. As a matter of fact, many wooden-handled boot knives can be converted to hand quarrels by simply drilling a small hole in the butt to fit dart vanes. If the handle is very light it should also be weighted with lead. For optimum efficiency, it is important that the lead be affixed to that part of the handle which is closest to the blade. Targets are the same as for the chakram, with the addition of the area directly beneath the heart.

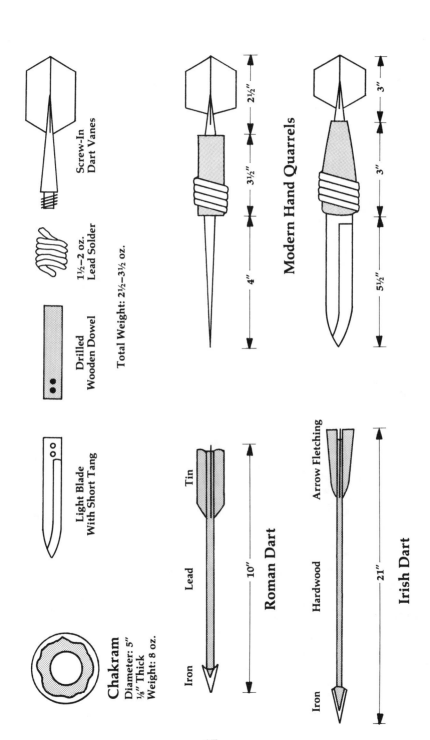

Screw-In
Dart Vanes

1½–2 oz.
Lead Solder

Drilled
Wooden Dowel

Total Weight: 2½–3½ oz.

Light Blade
With Short Tang

Chakram
Diameter: 5″
⅛″ Thick
Weight: 8 oz.

Modern Hand Quarrels

2½″ 3½″ 4″

3″ 3″ 5½″

Tin

Lead

Iron

10″

Roman Dart

Arrow Fletching

Hardwood

Iron

21″

Irish Dart